I CAN'T
FEEL
MY FACE

I CAN'T
FEEL
MY FACE

KRIS KIDD

A COLLABORATION WITH
THE ALTAR COLLECTIVE

First Edition: January 2014

ISBN-10: 1494317672
ISBN-13: 978-1494317676

Credits:
Cover photo by Katherine Hogan
Cover design by Katherine Hogan
Header images © Kris Kidd 2009-2013

www.thealtarcollective.com

CONTENTS:

For me

"That can't be him. What is he doing? Is he on something?"

I stare at the lanky figure; he is running around the room like a bat out of hell. His laughter roars across the room, reaching me at the doorway, pulling me towards him. I immediately begin to wonder what I have gotten myself into. We met through a mutual friend, and after a brief correspondence on Facebook— or maybe it was Twitter— we decided to meet up at our friend's charity event to discuss potential creative projects. He spots me and flings his skinny arms in the air, running towards me as though we have been friends for years. He wraps his arms around me, and his protruding hipbones dig into my t-shirt. He welcomes me in, and then falls to his knees, as though on cue. He is small, frail, his rib cage is burrowed in the seams of a designer tank top. He scrambles to his feet and asks if anybody has seen his phone.

This was my first impression of Kris Kidd, and it was only the start of what was to come. I first met Kris when he was at the naïve age of fifteen, and I had no way of knowing what was about to happen in his life. He was just months shy of his upcoming breakdown. Within the year, he would lose forty pounds, he would lose his father, and he would lose his mind.

Throughout the years, I have watched him fall apart and put himself back together again. From Los Angeles to New York, and then back again, I've watched his breakdowns unfold as many others do— in small "140 characters or less" excerpts. However, I have also had the unique opportunity to hear his story in all of its full, uncensored glory—be it over a brief coffee meeting, or in between heavy, drunken sobs during a last-minute photo shoot.

When Chelsea Kirk and I started The Altar Collective, we wanted to provide an outlet for aspiring writers to be heard and to be recognized. The collaboration with Kris was a perfect fit. I wanted to preserve his story in full, the way I had heard it before, and he wanted a forum in which he could tell his story. What followed was a fervent effort to capture all of the ups and downs, the hazy nights and the better days.

Kris is the American youth as seen through a funhouse mirror – fractured and disjointed. Almost caricature-like in his mannerisms, he is either the most brutally honest, or the most frighteningly comedic depiction of the current generation that has been seen yet. This collection of essays is a rare, unfiltered insight into his psyche for the public.

To hell and back— and then back to hell again for a brief cameo at a party— these essays reveal how far Kris has come in the past five years, although I still don't think he knows where his phone is.

BETWEEN SEASONS

Before we get started, I'd like to make two things

known:

1. If you ever happen to come in contact with someone who feels the need to describe me as "drunk" or "sloppy," you can rest assured that the word they were actually looking for was "festive."

2. It is fiscally imprudent *not* to drink your entire body weight in assorted mixed drinks when you hear the words "Open Bar."

Okay. There. I feel like we know each other better already.

* * *

It's 2009, a Thursday night in September, and I've stopped looking for stars in the Los Angeles sky. I settle instead for the ones I see in my head when I go three or four days without eating. Same difference.

Now, this could be just about any night, like, ever. Thursday is Sunday, October is April, and as far as I'm fucking concerned, it's *still* 2009. I don't really know anymore. I guess I could check a calendar, or something, but are you really going to make me go through the effort of checking my phone?

Wait a second. *Shit*. HAS ANYBODY SEEN MY PHONE?

This is a cycle. This is routine now. I am the product of a painfully adequate home— picket fences and red doors, and all that shit. I don't need you to show me any ink blotches because I know exactly what I am, and I did this to myself.

I'm on the rooftop of the W, sucking a Parliament down to its hollow filter and explaining to my friend's business manager that this is all just a very big misunderstanding— I quit smoking. "And can I have another glass of champagne please?" This is a Saturday in August, I think.

Therapy is dope because it gives me all the time I need to gnaw at the skin around my fingernails and ponder over whether or not I've ever been molested. On a Saturday morning, I'm sprawled out on the cheap, tear-stained carpeting in my therapist's office. My left thumb is chewed raw and bleeding, and I'm wondering who touched me. Like, when? And where?

It's February, and I'm in the checkout line at my local supermarket. I'm mumbling something about the calorie-count in Starburst fruit-chews, and my friend is holding a box of tinfoil to her chest like it's her own stillborn. The two of us are like clockwork— everyday in the same checkout line, with the same box of tinfoil and two 20oz cans of sugar-free Redbull, like we run some sort of nocturnal bakery, or something.

I snort six lines of Suboxone on a Tuesday in November, and to be honest, I'm not really sure what Suboxone is, but it smells like I just inhaled an orange grove, and I'm already starting to lose feeling in my face. I mix a thermos full of Sprite and UV blue, and I'm ready to go.

It's a Sunday night in late July, and I'm kneeling next to my father in the wet grass of our backyard with my hands pump-pump-pumping away at his hollow chest. My palms leave bright-red stains— too bright to be real— in the soft fabric of his t-shirt, and the cold night air smells like it does in my lucid dreams.

On a Monday or Friday in May or December, I'm wandering the aisles of a CVS in West Hollywood. I take lazy sips from a bottle of Fiji water filled to the brim with Barefoot Riesling, and I *think* I'm shopping for cleaning supplies? I'm not sure. I don't even have my own house to clean. What year is it? Who are you? FUCK.

Los Angeles has no seasons, so it's kind of hard to keep track of time here. The lines between spring, summer, fall, and winter all blur like my vision. I get stuck on repeat for different measures of eternity.

I'm constantly on some "Hi, I'm Kris, It's so nice to meet you" shit— even though I've already met the person, like, six fucking times. But it's not my fault. I'm not trying to be rude; I just genuinely don't remember. It's a constant state of blackout.

My fingers are blistered and they smell like lighter fluid— like burnt tin foil and rusted silverware. Quick question: Is it still considered heroin chic if I'm actually using heroin? No? *Whatever.*

I dye my jeans jet black once a week, but they never seem dark enough. I bleach my hair bright white twice a month but it never seems light enough. I drink two and a half bottles of champagne every night but I never seem drunk enough. And I know I'm not high enough until someone grabs my face to check my vision to see if I'm still responsive— And even then, I'm thinking to myself that I should probably do one more line, you know, *just to be safe.*

It's a Wednesday night in July, and I'm in the backseat of a speeding car somewhere on the outskirts of downtown LA. I'm hanging out the window and screaming at passers by in between fruitless drags of an unlit cigarette. Every five or six seconds, the car passes beneath a streetlight, and the entire car is illuminated. I smile. In this momentary burst of orange light, I can see everything. The dark is lifted and, even if it's just for a second, I feel complete.

The light leaves just as swiftly as it came, and then it's back to darkness— back to rooftops and grocery stores. Back to empty bedrooms and crowded dance floors. Back to getting high, and sinking low, back to getting drunk when I have nowhere to go. I sit in the backseat, impatient in the darkness, and I wait for the next burst of light.

And, to be clear, this doesn't necessarily have to be a Wednesday in July. This doesn't really have to be any time, or any place. This is me. This is me on any given day, of any month, of any year. This is me caught between seasons. This is me all the time, every time, and I really am *almost* sorry.

* * *

Okay. There. I feel like we know each other better already.

I GET IT NOW

In Los Angeles, everything is 100% organic, except the people. If it's not Gluten-free, you're not doing it right. If you've found yourself in a Kombucha aisle, and you can't afford it, then you're a long way from 7th and San Pedro—but *Namaste* anyway. If you hear the languid voice of Enya blaring from just outside your ears' peripherals, don't worry.

You're not dead; you're just dangerously close to a Hot Yoga workshop.

I need to move. I don't fit in here. I almost tried a juice cleanse once, but quickly remembered that I could starve, and was starving, myself for free.

I'm at yet another rooftop pool, and my face is freckled red from the sun, but I don't feel it because I've been playing scientist with Adderall and mimosas again. Silly me. It used to be that a few bumps of Adderall left me feeling really on top of things, but nowadays my hands shake and I get a little dizzy if I stand up too quickly. It's like, 3pm— 5'oclock God only knows where, and I have to tuck my phone in someone's purse just to keep myself from drunk-dialing my agent.

Pools here are weird because no one ever swims in them. No one really *does* anything here. We all just pretend to interact with our surroundings. All the girls drink Bacardi and hop parties. And junkie boys write songs for drunk girls with eyes starry. We've all got DUI's and UTI's and we smoke weed to chill when we get too high.

The homeless dudes on Alameda all have legs any runway model would kill for, and sometimes I think of giving them money, but— I don't know, I've got bills to not pay, and drinks to make people buy for me.

I'm losing sleep. Places like Drai's, Cinespace, and L Bar all bore me now. I won't legally be able to enter them for six years, but you get what I'm saying.

In a daze at Drai's.

Vodka doused at Soho House.

Out of place at Cinespace.

Knowing the drill is a skill

when you can't pay your bills.

Everywhere I go, I kind of half stumble, half stomp. If there's a balcony within a hundred feet of me at any given time, I am on it— smoking a Marlboro light 100 and complaining about something. I am very Californian. My skin is tan, and I'm always half asleep. Sometimes, if I'm high enough, the Red Hot Chili Peppers make me cry, but only because they *get* me, you know?

You can always see my pulse, and my bones make weird cracking noises if I do anything too strenuous. There is almost always someone next to me force feeding me water because I am almost always hung-over, and if I'm not, I'm still drunk.

I always leave my spare change in the little charity boxes when I'm buying cigarettes at 7-11— you know, the ones with the pictures of starving children, children with cancer, children with distended bellies who wear rags and are covered in flies… Not because I care about them, but because I hate loose change.

I make anyone who drives me home late at night sit on my couch in the dark and watch at least one episode of *Jersey Shore* with me on Netflix while I binge eat. 'Round come sunrise, I'm still watching Netflix, *Rugrats* now— stuffing myself with Dreyer's chocolate ice-cream, and taking thirty-minute breaks before vomiting. I stumble around the house for the rest of the day, feeling comfort in my loneliness, and all the while feeling terribly alone.

See, that's the thing about L.A.— When you've mastered the art of feeling lonely in a room full of people, that's when you know. When you have to excuse yourself from polite conversation with people who are two, maybe three, times your age just to hide in a bathroom stall for hours at a time, that's when it really hits you. Once you've snorted a line off of just about every reflective surface in West Hollywood, you just get it.

I'm at a release party in downtown when my nose

begins to bleed. The stale air in the studio smells like kale and vodka, and I make my way to the bathroom to clean up after myself. A bag of bones can slip through small cracks in a crowd effortlessly. Twisting and turning every so often, cutting myself down to size, I slink between hushed murmurs that a Disney channel star has just arrived. She's already drunk, and everyone is taking pictures. *Flash!*

Floating in a radioactive sea of cell phone screens, I look down to see a small red droplet flowering in the thin, white fabric of my t-shirt. *Flash!* The first drop is followed by another, and then another. On the opposite end of the studio, the Disney star is snarling at the communal flash of cell phones in the crowd, barking like a dog at the end of its leash. *Flash!* I avert my gaze, and look down at my t-shirt, now a crimson mess of Pollock proportions. *Flash!* Nobody is noticing.

And I get that.

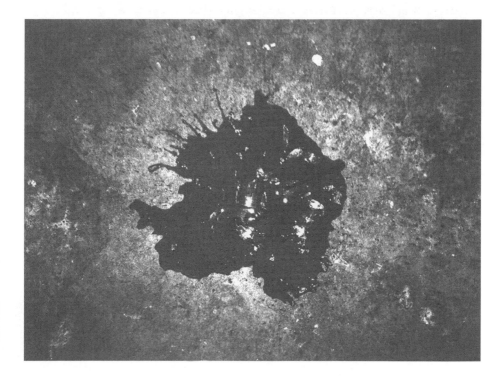

THE MEAT MARKET

It's Sunday night and I'm at Greenhouse, a deliriously chic and surprisingly eco-friendly gay club in Soho. The walls and ceiling on the first floor are covered in ivy, and I can't help but feel very tribal and grounded. The second floor is covered in crystals and refracted light, like— imagine a snow palace, but on acid. There you go. That's it. That's the second floor at Greenhouse.

I was never really all that into clubs, but when you're just old enough to drive a car, and the people you surround yourself with are just old enough to *rent* one, it's kind of what you have to do.

My friends and I order drinks in the jungle downstairs before upgrading to the glass castle. Once on the second floor, we snag a booth in the back and I check the time on my phone.

It's 11:36. Back in Los Angeles, three hours ago and oh-so-far away, my mother is probably getting ready to go to sleep. I wonder if she misses me. Is she thinking about me? My mother hasn't seen my face between the hours of 10 pm and 5 am in years, so I highly doubt it, but it is nice to think about— Someone pulls me by the arm and whisks me away to dance.

I'm starved, hollow, and the pills in my empty stomach make me feel like a maraca when I dance. My hands shake, and my head hurts, and all of this is just a few months before David Guetta became a thing and *Sexy Bitch* became the compliment of a generation, so the club is playing some limited release Ying Yang Twins song to pass the time.

SO TAKE YA CLOTHES OFF, GET NAKED/ IT TOOK YA MOMMA NINE MONTHS TO MAKE IT/ AND YES I LOVE SEEIN' YOU SHAKE IT

I spill my drink.

BEND YA BACK, GIRL, GO ON, BREAK IT/ KEEP IT REAL, GIRL, DON'T FAKE IT/ IF YOU WANTED MONEY, GO ON, TAKE IT

I check my nose for blood by lightly brushing my nostrils with the pads of my fingers. I'm in the clear, but I'm short a drink. The friends I came with are gone. They found a socialite to lust over and left me on the dance floor.

I spot them in the VIP section and begin to slither

toward them when a go-go dancer darts out in front of me —
late for his shift, or something. He is covered in glitter and
grease, like a homoerotic water nymph, and it's all just so
fitting in the crystal ballroom. I watch as he finds his perch
on the stage, and begins to gyrate like a broken washing
machine.

I scoff, and turn on my heel, heading back toward the
VIP area. The Ying Yang Twins have said their goodbyes
and are replaced by a frustratingly catchy Diplo-crafted
mash up of Peter Bjorn & John's *Young Folks*, and *Candy*
by The Pack.

IF YOU KNEW MY STORY WORD FOR WORD/
HAD ALL OF MY HISTORY/ WOULD YOU GO ALONG
WITH SOMEONE LIKE ME?

A small, leather-skinned man with his shirt all the
way unbuttoned keeps making eye contact with me from
across the room. He sweats like a mechanic and smiles like a

dentist.

IT'S MY PUSSY, I CAN DO WHAT I WANT/ HMPH, I'M A BIG GIRL NOW/

I can tell that the mechanic/dentist-hybrid is fantasizing about me, and I wonder if he can tell that I am fantasizing about him too. I imagine him bringing me a drink and then, like, leaving me alone… but you know, *you can't always get what you want*, and all that shit.

I give the mechanic/dentist-hybrid the finger and quickly retreat to the VIP section. When I arrive, it's a velvet-rope catastrophe. A barrel-chested bouncer that I can only assume is called "Ice," or "Trigger," or something, blocks the entry.

"Oh, I'm with them…" I mumble, pointing to a binge-drinking huddle of blondes in a corner booth.

"No, he's with me."

What sounds like a cartoon pig turns out to be a large,

rotund man in an Armani suit.

I shake my head in disagreement, but the man-pig insists.

Ice, or Trigger, or whatever, steps out of the way, and I am escorted into the VIP area.

"Do you come here often?"

I stifle a laugh. My eyes lock on a bottle of champagne on man-pig's table, and I pour myself a glass.

"You are a beautiful, beautiful boy."

"Thanksssss." I hiss.

"You know, I host Sunday nights here…"

"That's super dope," I interject. "But I really should be getting back to my friends. They're missing me, I'm sure."

The pile of blondes in the corner unite in an uproar of laughter, and I turn to face the man-pig. "Nice meeting you."

"Wait." He grabs my arm. "Do you dance?"

"Excuse me?" I wrestle out of his grip.

"I'm sorry, you're just such a beautiful boy."

Some Steve Buscemi-looking slime ball from man-pig's table repeats the word "beautiful" in a Percocet drawl.

"Yeah, okay, we covered that. What do you want?" I take a drink.

Man-pig laughs. "We'd love to have you dance for us."

"Right now?"

Man-pig laughs again, and Buschemi-slime slumps down in his seat.

"No, I mean, we'd love to have you dance here on Sunday nights." He gestures out to the stage, his sausage fingers pointed at the glittering array of underage go-go dancers.

"Well, I'm only here for another few days, so..."

"Such a shame," Man-pig sighs. "Have you ever

thought of moving here? We could help you get situated, you know, get your feet on the ground."

I look down at my feet at then up at the man-pig. He's smiling, and it's weird. I glance over my shoulder at the go-go dancers, sweating for a crowd of hundreds of men just like the man-pig. I shudder at the thought. Taking the last swig of my champagne, I set the glass down on the table. "It was nice talking to you."

I stumble over to the blondes, and I slide into their booth. They're in the middle of a heart-to-heart discussion about their experiences with Xanax.

"It's like, nice, because I'm always so stressed, you know? Like, you know me. I'm always stressed. Xanax, like, helps me relax."

I try to follow, but one of the blondes begins talking about Tequila, and I lose focus. I check my phone. It is 12:03. By now, my mother is dead asleep in Los Angeles, and my father— well, he's just dead. I spy an unattended

drink and snatch it quickly. I toss the stirrers on the ground

and chug. Vodka soda. Gross, but, *beggars can't be*

choosers, or whatever.

"But if you mix Xanax and Tequila? Let me tell

you…"

I close my eyes and think of a time before nightclubs

and weird old men, a time before Xanax and Tequila, before

Percocets and vodka. And, to be honest, if weed is a

gateway drug, then I really did hop the fence, but sometimes

I can't help but miss the sticky-sweet warmth of a good old

fashioned hot box. I think of eighth grade, taking half-

hearted hits in the backseat of a car parked just three blocks

from my house— with my dad still alive, and my mom still

worrying.

"Bitch, did you finish my drink?" The blondes have

finished their seminar on Xanax and Tequila. "It's time to

go."

I evacuate the VIP area in a cloud of white-blonde clip-in extensions, with my eyes locked on the stage. I watch as one of the dancers begins to slow down— he is tired, weak. His two-step seems lifeless, his face dull. He has sweated off his glitter, and everything left of him is a reflex. His vital signs flicker like the strobe lights above us. His body is here, but his mind is elsewhere— just a puppet, a piece of meat, up for sale. *Pathetic*, I think to myself as my friends pay the tab.

A week later, I'm in Brooklyn, shooting for the premiere issue of some under-budget, up-and-coming men's fashion magazine. Sprawled out on the photographer's mattress with my clothes lying in a heap somewhere in the kitchen, I pull the waistband of my briefs down to expose my hipbones, and I think of home.

FRUIT ROLL-UPS

Where I am now is the backseat of a parked '98 Subaru

Impreza—red, the color of dried blood, and probably

stolen— trying to light a cigarette. I'm alone in the car, and

even after my frantic search through the front and back

seats— glove box included— the only cigarette I can find is

a Kool 100. This really pisses me off, but I've already

smoked my pack (Marlboro Lights, in case you were wondering), and I'm desperate.

I fumble with my lighter, my hands shaking feverishly, and just as I finally achieve a spark, the passenger door to my right is thrown open. A large, black hand flies into the backseat and swats the lighter out of my hand.

"Fuck you thinkin', trick? That's a white lighter. Get that shit out the car."

It's Mac. I just met Mac tonight, and I can already tell we are *not* going to see eye to eye. He reaches down past my knobby knees, grabs the lighter, and tosses it out into the street. I ask him what the color of my lighter has to do with anything, and he tells me that white lighters are bad luck. He tells me that everybody knows that.

"Well, to be fair, I was using it to light a cigarette, so I guess dying is just sort of a part of my plan..." It's dark outside, but I'm pretty sure I can see Mac's eyes rolling. He calls me crazy.

"Where is everybody?" I ask. My teeth are chattering, and I'm genuinely wondering what Mac's next move would be if I got out of the car to retrieve the white lighter.

"Man, be patient. Phase is just makin' sure the shit's good before he buys it. They'll be here in a minute."

Mac, Phase: everyone here is of the we-don't-use-real-names-here mentality, so most of the time I feel like a really pilled up Snow White rolling around in the hood with seven drug-dealing dwarves—which, I don't know… these things are never really as fun as they sound like they'd be.

I'm chewing on the filter end of my last resort Kool 100 when Phase emerges from the apartment complex with his crew in tow, his hands rustling in the pockets of his basketball shorts. Phase slithers into the passenger seat, Mac takes the wheel, and the other three— Freight, Citrus, and

Fault — squeeze into the backseat, trapping me in the middle.

"Did you have a nice stay?" I sigh as we pull away from the curb.

"Huh?" Phase looks over his shoulder to face me. He's already packing a bowl.

"You were in there for, like, an hour." I reach over to snatch the lighter from his left hand, but he jerks away.

"Man, chill," he laughs. "We were only in there for a minute. Besides, we picked up a shitload. We had to make sure that shit was legit-i-mate."

"And?" I ask. "Is it legitimate?"

"Idunno, man. Shit hasn't kicked in yet, but there was some bitch in there that popped two a couple hours ago, and she was *on one*. You saw that shit, man." He gestures to Citrus, who nods, laughing. "She was feelin' good."

"Well, she sounds precious." I reach again for the lighter, but Phase leans over me and passes it to Fault.

Phase then hands everyone in the back seat but me a small, round pill. Fault and Citrus swallow it dry, and Freight reaches under the seat to retrieve a Miller High Life. He unscrews the cap, takes the hit, and washes it down with the stale beer. Phase asks if I want one, and I kick the back of his seat.

"I hope to God that's a fucking joke, Phase." I reach out to Fault to grab the lighter, but he slides it into the left pocket of his Rocawear jeans. I stick the unlit cigarette in my mouth and puff it fruitlessly to pass the time.

I was fifteen the first time I met Phase. We were at a party, and after a few minutes of talking, he offered me a pill. My coke brain tricked me into reaching for it, but it was my well-educated, suburban brain that stopped me in my tracks.

"What is it?" I coughed.

"It's X, man. Take it. It's yours."

"Oh. No thank you," I mumbled, handing it back to him. "I don't do fun drugs."

We both laughed.

"Fuck is that supposed to mean? You blown right now, aren't you?"

"Oh, definitely. But that's only to keep my ballerina-thin figure."

Phase laughed, taking the X for himself. "You're a trip, man."

Three parties and twelve nosebleeds later, Phase had shown me all of his rap demos, and I had told him all about my life in Los Angeles— my child acting, my budding modeling career, my affinity for appetite suppressants. But

Phase's favorite thing to talk about was the Fruit Roll-Ups commercial I booked when I was nine. He found it on YouTube within minutes.

"Man, I remember that shit!" He laughed, bleeding pot smoke. "Fuckin' trippy. I can't believe that's you! Look at you, all happy and shit."

At every party we ever went to, he'd bring up the commercial. It became my thing— my claim to fame. I was the Fruit Roll-Ups kid. We couldn't go anywhere without another person approaching us and asking, "Yo, aren't you that Fruit Loops guy?"

"Well, actually, it was Fruit Roll-Ups, but—"

"Bro, that's so sick. You all famous and shit? You got money?"

I was a part of Phase's traveling circus. I was the kid who was on TV that one time.

"Hey, I hear you was in a Fruity Pebbles commercial?"

"Yeah, I mean, it was for Fruit Roll-Ups, but I—"

"Yo, that's tight!"

At a party in North Long Beach, a tall, wiry man they called Knight stopped Phase in the middle of telling the story.

"Naw, I call bullshit. This lil' bitch don't look like he could be in a commercial for fruit snacks, or some shit. He's all cracked out."

Silence.

"Well, I was nine, so I was doing a little less coke then."

Phase laughed, and everyone followed suit, including Knight, who reached his fist out for me to pound it. Self-awareness is key.

Back in the dried-blood Impreza, everyone is laughing. Everyone but me, that is. Their X kicks in around the same time as my comedown, and I just want to go home. I'm rifling through the pockets of my leather jacket, every zipper getting caught on something. It's 5am, and we're in the parking lot of an elementary school in Lakewood, waiting for Mac while he takes a piss. Dead Prez is playing on the car's stereo, telling me that it's bigger than Hip-Hop, but I beg to differ. My head hurts and I can feel the soft onset of a heavy nosebleed.

"What's the plan?" I ask, my fingers clutching a gram bag in the recesses of my jacket pocket. "Like, what are we doing?" I pause, the unlit cigarette still hanging from my mouth, "And for the love of God will someone please give me a *fucking* lighter?"

"No, bitch. You steal lighters. No one trusts you." He continues, ignoring me. "Fault wants us to drop him off at some bitch's house and then we probably just gonna go kick it at my place," Phase says, taking the last gulp of his Four Loko.

"Fuck it," I pour the remaining contents of the bag out onto the back of my left hand, fashioning a small bump. "But I need, like, a drink, or something. Do you have any vodka at the house?"

"Naw, man. I got some 40's though."

My left hand in the air, the right already pressed against my nostril, I scoff. "Whatever."

Mac jumps back into the car, and I snort the bump hastily. His face is pale, or, as pale as it can get when you're black, I guess.

"What's wrong, bro?"

"Five-O around the corner; ya'all need to get down, for real." Mac tucks his head between his knees, and everyone else in the car does the same.

I sit up straight for a moment, a buoy in a sea of terrified thugs.

"Are we really? Is this really? I can *not* handle this shit right now." I duck, and the gram bag falls from my lap, floating to my feet— a lone snowflake.

The cop car passes swiftly, silently, and once Mac is sure it is long gone, he sits upright, and starts the car.

"What in the *fuck* was that all about?" I groan as we exit the parking lot.

"Mac's just sketched 'cause he shot somebody yesterday." Citrus breaks the silence. "It was all over the news and shit. Fuckin' crazy."

The rest of the car ride is silent. On the stereo, Ice Cube says it was a good day— says he didn't even have to use his AK— but, again, I must beg to differ. When we arrive at Fault's bitch's place, I exit the car with him.

"Phase, can I talk to you?"

Phase shuts the car door behind him and stumbles over to me. "Wassup, bro?"

"I want to go home. I did *not* sign up for this shit. You want to rap? That's cool. You want to sling X and smoke weed and fuck shit up, that's fine. But I do *not* want to kick it with a fucking murderer."

Phase laughs.

"Alright, man. Listen." He cups his fist in his hand. "I like you. You're chill. But all this pansy shit has got to stop. You wanna kick it with thugs and shit, and act all hard? Then you gotta be hard. You can't be actin' like a little bitch when shit gets crazy. 'Cause that's what you're acting like right now. A little pussy bitch."

I try and think of something to say, a witty response that only a well-educated kid from the suburbs could come up with, but I am empty. Staring at Phase in the dull grey light of an impending sunrise, the novelty has faded. The idyllic mayhem of two cultures colliding just doesn't seem as funny anymore. The lower class meets the upper middle. The gangster meets the coke fiend. I want to think that my thoughts and actions are genuine, but the fact of the matter is that everything just seems so much "bigger" on TV.

"Just take me home."

When we arrive at my house, it's difficult not to admire its picturesque beauty: The perfectly manicured lawn and accompanying rose bushes, the bright red door, the gram bag hidden somewhere in the recesses of my sock drawer...

"Get the fuck out my car," Mac barks.

"It's been fun, guys. Drive safe." I try and do that whole double-pat thing on the roof of the car, but it peels away beneath my palm.

I step out of the car and up onto the curb. They're already turning the corner, and in the early morning light, with the sun glowing behind the rooftops of all the houses, the car's dried-blood paintjob looks a little more vibrant— a little more alive. My unlit cigarette shakes in my hand. I stare at it blankly. There are a million stolen lighters hidden next to the gram bag in my sock drawer. I'm over it.

My head throbs, and my gaze crawls up the street. Every window in every house is illuminated, flickering with the hazy blue light of morning television. I imagine each household basking in the quiet feedback of the morning news.

A young man was killed last night in a drive-by shooting.

A liquor store, robbed at gunpoint.

Then, a commercial break. Probably selling fruit snacks. Or some shit.

KO PHI PHI

At a "studio" in the valley, I ask for my money in a
hazy fervor that borders on hysteria, or maybe the fringe of
what could be a chemical calm. One-hundred-three pounds,
teeny-tiny, and covered in coke like a moth in dust, I ask for
my money, so I can leave this place and go somewhere
foreign, and distant, and cheap. Somewhere where the
mountain ranges can become mirror images of the bones in

my back. I'll find a little shack on the beach, and I'll swim every day, and maybe bartend at night, making fake friends to pass the time.

At this "studio" in the valley—which is really just an empty warehouse if we're being technical— a man in an outdated Marc Jacobs blazer hands me a thin stack of hundred dollar bills, and I immediately retreat to the bathroom.

I've memorized the best angles in the bathroom mirror from which to see how badly I've disintegrated. I truly do go from sixty to zero. I am bitter… cold. I was halfhearted a year ago, but I can no longer calculate the fraction of what's left. I watch in the mirror, my head cocked over my shoulder so as to see my shoulder blade now covered in a layer of fat I can't quite manage. I scream. A lot. At least once a day, and I scroll through my phone's contact list at least twice. I throw my phone across the room in defeat three times a day minimum.

I have distanced myself from everyone, and I have no reason to be as angry as I am because I brought this on myself, and I don't need you to tell me that because I've already heard it in my head for the billionth time today. Hunched over in the mirror, curving in on myself, I watch my thighs touch, and I might scream again, or I might decide to keep it internal for once and let it trickle through my lungs and the lining of my stomach.

In the mirror I stand, an injured deer in headlights, or maybe high beams, judging by the way my eyes water. I measure my wrists with my fingers, and I clutch at my rib cage, fingering it languidly, tracing the rise and fall of sharp bones until my heartbeat slows, and I dream of a faraway ocean.

I dream of bony mountains and quiet seas, and I dream of a party in bloom at dusk that can be heard from my little shack on the beach. With my head in the toilet for the billionth time today— gagging on my fingers on another worst day of another worst month, of another worst year— I use my free hand to count my money, and I dream of a physical detachment from this world to rival the one I feel in the pit of my stomach every day.

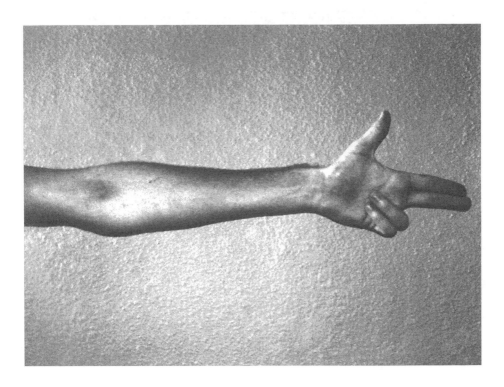

BALLOON ANIMALS

In June of 2009, I tell my father to kill himself. We're standing in the kitchen, and he's crying and I'm wearing a $300 sweater with, like, an oversized hood sort of thing going on, holding the biggest knife I can find. It's all *very* avant-garde.

In July of 2009, my father blows his brains out in the backyard. I'm in the kitchen, deciding what color I'm going to dye my hair (my father never let me), and watching through the window as he is zipped into a body bag.

I know it sounds a bit trite, but I really do get everything I want now. They say life is a game, and I guess I might agree if the stakes were a little higher, but it's just so *easy* to fall into a cycle. I get bored.

I bleach my hair bright white in the city of Compton within weeks of my father's suicide. My hands fidget, drumming my fingers against my sternum and listening to the metallic whir of my cocaine heart.

In Irvine, or Costa Mesa, or whatever, my therapist tries her very best to avoid the word "manipulative" at all costs, but I catch on quickly and I give her a free pass. I pick a bleach-scab from my scalp, and tell her it's true. She keeps mints on her desk, and every time I leave, I take a handful, and then another. I forgive myself each time, telling her she should be happy I'm eating anything at all. She is never as impressed as I want her to be.

I buy six bottles of wine at *5 O'clock Liquor* in the city of Bell, using an expired I.D. I stole from a friend-of-a-friend-of-an-acquaintance in New York. The man on the I.D. is four inches shorter, and fifty pounds heavier than I am, and I explain to Rajan, the cashier, that I've been losing weight lately due to stress. I make sad eyes, and shift my weight from foot to foot while he sighs and continues to ring me up.

I'm like those Jeff Koons pieces— the balloon animals— all shiny and pretty, but hollow on the inside. I'm half-high, taking pictures of myself on my MacBook's photo booth while Joy Division's *Disorder* plays over and over again in my iTunes library.

My friend decides to go to rehab— to get clean or to take a vacation, I can't remember which, and I throw all her paraphernalia into a dumpster and stuff her Xanax into my back pocket, because I am a saint.

I'm back at *5 O'clock Liquor,* wearing a distressed Calvin Klein muscle-tee and setting a 40oz of Miller High Life on the counter next to a bag of gummy worms. This cashier's name is Sanjiv. He takes one look at the I.D. and tells me he can't sell me the beer. WHERE THE FUCK IS RAJAN? I slam my fists on the counter. Sanjiv is not at all amused. RAJAN SELLS ME BEER EVERY TIME I COME HERE! DO YOU WANT TO LOSE YOUR FUCKING LIQUOR LICENSE? I'm crying now. CALL RAJAN! I WANT TO SPEAK TO RAJAN! I WILL FUCKING REPORT YOU!

It's just that easy.

At three in the morning, I smell like champagne and Colgate, wandering the streets of downtown and playing don't-step-on-the-cracks, waiting for the trains to start running again. Little L.A. waif waits, wastes. I'm losing sight, smell, and taste. I'd hail a cab, but they never pick me up. They don't trust me. I stand at the intersection of Flower and 6th, holding a wad of cash in the air, and the cabs still avoid me. I'm Julia fucking Roberts.

I'm posing for a high school art class, shivering like a Grand-mal seizure, and I take my shirt off, even though the teacher specifically asked me not to during our fifteen minute briefing. Nobody compliments me on the extreme visibility of my ribcage, so I ask the class what they think about it.

I'm at The Standard on Sunset with a producer I met on a shoot, wearing a leather jacket I stole from an acquaintance-of-a-friend-of-a-friend, and the producer says he wants to go out for dinner. I tell him I'd rather have drinks, and of course he complies. I make sure to remind him that I have no money in between every gulp of my six or seven vodka-Redbulls.

"IS THIS REALLY A 'ME' ISSUE?" I'm screaming at my mom in the kitchen because she won't stop asking me where I go at night. I'm wearing a ninety dollar tank top that I practically begged the designer for, and the gold-foil lettering shimmers when I stomp my feet on the ground.

I am the cause of the energy crisis. When the sun sets, I turn all of the lights on, and I keep them on until the sun returns. Darkness equates to loneliness and I have, over the years, developed a Motel 6 mentality. I bask in late-night artificial light and amphetamine clarity, dancing to *There Is a Light That Never Goes Out* by The Smiths and waiting for morning to come.

I drink Coke-zero while I score coke from an honors student in Huntington Beach. I take my sweet time gumming

it at home while listening to the Runaways' *Cherry Bomb*,
hyping myself up for another night alone.

"I'm just not into this," I declare during my last
therapy session when my therapist asks if I resent my father
for killing himself. Then I dump her entire bowl of mints
into my backpack and leave.

The game is getting old, and I don't know if it's
because I've mastered the art of it, or if I just have some
weird attention-deficit-disorder when it comes to getting my
way all the time, every time. My nose bleeds, and every
comedown feels like an overdose. I try to make peace with
God each time, but he shows no interest, and it reminds me
of my dad, and I get so upset that I just *have* to do another
line. Like I said, a cycle.

In my kitchen, I'm staring out the window at the
impending storm clouds, and pretending to wash dishes—
which I really don't think is fair because I never eat any of

the food here. In the backyard, there is a small patch of dead grass where my father's head laid the night he killed himself. I feel a pinch on the palm of my hand and look down to see that I'm bleeding. I pull the big knife out of the sink and rinse the blade off in the running water.

It's raining outside now. The sky is dirty blue. Mud begins to puddle in the little patch of dead-dad grass, and I wonder if anything will ever grow there again.

ACKNOWLEDGEMENTS:

I would like to thank, first and foremost, Katherine Hogan and Chelsea Kirk of The Altar Collective for taking a chance on publishing my strange little collection of work. The process has been incredible, and without them, this never would have happened.

I would also like to thank my lovely editor and mentor, Lisa Montagne, for helping me learn to take control of my abstract thoughts, for keeping me grounded, and for always pushing me to become a better writer.

Last, but certainly not least, I want to thank the friends and family that stand by me to this day— they saw this story unfold with their own eyes, and stuck around to see me through it. For that, I am eternally grateful.

(Author photograph © Ari Abramczyk)

I Can't Feel My Face is Kris Kidd's first published collection of work. He lives in Los Angeles, California, and should be considered armed and extremely dangerous.

Made in the USA
Middletown, DE
20 March 2015